choose to l

a poem about life, love, and

by c. kevin wanzer

artwork by kristin tuller

A Poem about life, love and choices

First edition published by February 2006 by AuthorHouse
Second edition published February 2015 by Choose to Love, LLC

Poem by C. Kevin Wanzer
Artwork by Kristin Tuller
Book design by C. Kevin Wanzer Akamu and Matthew Vire
Printed in Malaysia.

Can you find the hearts? There is one in every illustration.
Find the answers at ChooseToLove.com.

ISBN-13: 978-163315295-3

for scout
(what time is it?)

and for all who
choose to love

it is amazing
in this world today

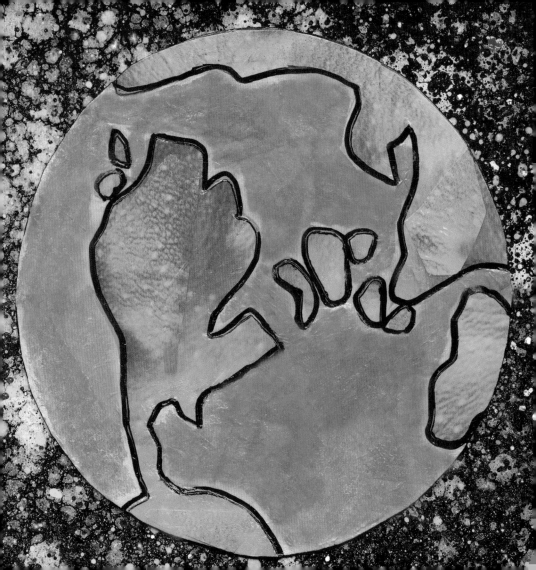

filled with
love and hate

what separates the common one from the one who is truly great

for it's not the wealth
in your bank account

or the possessions in
your own back yard

it is instead
what you share from
inside of your
loving, caring heart

you do not choose
your color of skin,
you don't choose
to be born rich or poor

you do not choose
to be deaf or blind,
wishing you had
something more

you do not choose
with whom you
fall in love, you don't
choose to be born
woman or man

you do not choose
your family at birth,
it's all part of a
much larger plan

and although for
some it's hard to relate
to the differences
others endure

keep in mind
there are certain
choices that make
you shallow or pure

you do
choose to love
or hate

you do
choose to follow
or lead

you do choose to
embrace or ignore
others in their
time of need

some things in life
you cannot change

but your
attitude can change;
it's true

and by doing so,
you can affect the
people who look
up to you

the meaning of life
is the greatest
mystery of all

but the answer
is easily found

it is unconditional love for ALL humankind

who walk on our
common ground

A Dream Come True:
The Creation of *Choose to Love*

Choose to Love is literally a dream come true. In 1992, while staying at a hotel room in Columbus, Georgia, Kevin Wanzer awoke from a dream in the middle of the night. He grabbed the hotel notepad by the side of his bed and quickly jotted down, verbatim, the poem that had come to him in his sleep.

Kevin kept the poem to himself for nearly fifteen years. Then he commissioned his artist friend, Kristin Tuller, to create original illustrations to accompany the poem in a book dedicated to his son, Scout. *Choose to Love* was originally published in 2006.

Now, Kevin's dream is for others to read and share the message with those they choose to love.

c. kevin wanzer

Kevin Wanzer has been empowering audiences – one laugh at a time – since his sophomore year of high school, by sharing his message of love, leadership, and laughter.

Kevin graduated with honors from Butler University in his hometown of Indianapolis, Indiana. While in college, Kevin served on the staff of *Late Night with David Letterman*, addressed the United Nations with the first lady of the United States, and became one of the nation's youngest presidential appointees in history.

Kevin's favorite place in the world is at home with his family.

kristin tuller

Kristin Tuller is a graduate of Indiana University with a degree in Social and Behavioral Sciences. She works privately as a mentor/facilitator for several individuals in addition to working as an artist. Friends with Kevin since childhood, she makes her home in Indianapolis.

Additional copies of this book
are available for purchase at
ChoosetoLove.com.

For information on booking Kevin to speak
for your company, school, or organization, visit
KevinWanzer.com.